MORE!

AWESOME
JOKES

6 EVERY VOL 2

YEAR OLD
SHOULD
KNOW!

Design: Fanni Williams / thehappycolourstudio.com
www.matwaugh.co.uk

Produced by Big Red Button Books,
a division of Say So Media Ltd.

ISBN: 978-1-912883-10-3

Published: July 2019

A note for parents and readers from the USA: I'm British. I can't help it. I'm a bloke
who goes on holiday for a fortnight, never uses a washroom and comes home knackered
I don't have a Scooby-Doo who the Red Sox are, or what I should do with a doohickey. I've
taken out any jokes about the Queen (sorry, Ma'am), but you may still find a few that
aren't your cup of tea. The rest? Hopefully they're the bee's knees!

MORE! MORE! MORE!
AWESOME JOKES
EVERY VOL 2
6 YEAR OLD SHOULD KNOW!

MAT WAUGH
ILLUSTRATIONS BY YURKO RYMAR

Hey – you're back!

Don't I remember you? Weren't you that kid I met, reading the first book of Awesome Jokes?

Wow. You're bigger. And I love your hair now. From down here on the page I can see up your nose, too.

So here we are again, back with a monster sack of fresh, squirming jokes. I caught them all myself, you know.

So pull out a wriggly one, let it go and see who laughs!

PS Got your own joke or want to write your own? See page 56!

↓Laughs start here↓

Where does a baker like to put her hair?
In a bun!

What question do you ask when somebody sneezes?
A tishoo?

What do you call a bee that goes 'oooooooooooh'?
A zom-bee!

Which dog has hands instead of paws?
A watchdog!

What does a pig use on a sore trotter?
Oinkment!

What do you call a girl who's impossible to find?
Heidi!

Why did the boy refuse to do his maths test?
He said he wanted to save it for a brainy day!

How do you stop a dog video?
Press the paws button!

How do birds drink?
From a beaker!

What do you call a fat shark?
Thick and fin!

How do crayfish draw?
With crayons, of course!

How do you make a scary sandwich?
Fill it with **SCREAM** cheese!

Why don't cats win races?
Because when they see a lap, they sit down!

Why would broccoli and carrot lemonade be good for you?
Because of all the vegeta-bubbles!

What key do you use to open a cow barn?
Mil-key!

Which bars do prisoners like best?
Chocolate bars!

What do cats take on holiday?
Passpawts!

 **DOCTOR, DOCTOR!** **Please help – I feel like I'm drowning! What should I do?**
Keep your chin up!

How do you call a camel?

By his thirst name!

What do you call a bunny on the lawn?
A grass hopper!

Knock Knock! Who's there?
Wood!
Wood who?
Wouldn't you like to know!

How do bees get to lessons?
On the school buzz!

 **I have a terrible memory.**
I know, you told me that when you came in this morning.

Why do you need slippers in Paddington's house?
Because of his hard stairs!

What do you call a broken toaster?
A bread-stick!

How does the lookout on a
pirate ship like his food?
Spy-see!

Which prison bars get smaller the more they're used?

Bars of soap!

 **It's so weird –
I feel like entering a
marathon!**
I'm sure you'll get
better in the long run!

What are twin kittens called?
Copy cats!

**What do you call a giraffe
with a sore throat?**
A massive pain in the neck!

**What do you call a
pirate's pet dog?**
Ship Rex!

What do you call a sticky hairbrush?
A honey comb!

How do you wrap a sandwich?
Use sandpaper!

How do you get ready for a storm?
Put on your thunderwear!

Which tree is easiest to roll?
Pastry!

What do you call a bug with jammy feet?
A *stick* insect!

DOCTOR, DOCTOR!

I feel dizzy, like I'm 20 stories up on a window ledge. Hang on, I'll be with you in ten minutes!

Which bird can cross rivers?
A spar-row! (or a crow!)

What do you call a bird that's been to the gym?
Puffin!

Every time I have a meal I drop my fork! Is that normal?
Oh no. I think it's time for you to get a grip!

What do band members eat for lunch?
Drum rolls!

What do you call a boy who falls over as soon as he gets up?
A day tripper!

How do you catch magpies?
With a magnet!

You must be joking!

HELP! I'm under attack! Six-year-olds from all over the world have sent me their funniest jokes. And what makes me grumpy is that they might be funnier than mine!

Think you can do better? See page 56!

KIERAN FROM HARROW, UK

What colour is the wind?

Blew!

AARON FROM ST ALBANS, UK

What do you call a cow that does karate?

Kung-foo moo!

TEDDY FROM EVANSTON, USA

How do you start a flower race?

Ready... Set... Grow!

RASHEED FROM LONDON, UK

Why are you late for school?

Because I had choco-late for breakfast!

LILA FROM PRINCETON, USA

Who lives on Pluto?

BENJAMIN FROM LONDON, UK

What did Santa say when he fell down the chimney?

Dwarves (because it's a dwarf planet, of course!)

Ho Ho... whoah!

SHILOH FROM GRANDVILLE, USA

Who brings Christmas presents to pigs?

ALEXANDER FROM RALEIGH, USA

How did the duck pay for his dinner?

Santa Hooves!

He put it on his bill!

DANIEL FROM BURTON ON TRENT, UK

What do you call Thumper without a thumb?

Per!

What time do you go to the dentists?

At tooth hurty – ha ha ha!

How do bats learn?

Because they go to school to learn the alphabat!

What do you call a baby without its baby toy?

A cry baby!

Knock, Knock!
Who's there?
Banana.
Banana who?
Knock, Knock!
Who's there?
Banana.
Banana who?
Knock, Knock!
Who's there?
Orange.
Orange who?
Orange you glad I didn't say banana again!

Knock, Knock!
Who's there?
Canoe.
Canoe who?
Canoe help me with my homework?

What did the 5 say to the person?

You can high 5 me if you want

Knock, Knock!
Who's there?
I don't know, go open the door and find out!

What do you call a tree with no legs?

A tree. Trees don't have legs.

Why did the cow do jumping jacks?

He wanted a milkshake!

Why did the egg tumble down the street?

He wanted to be an egg roll!

What do you call a nut that's made out of dough?

A doughnut!

Knock, Knock!
Who's there?
Dog.
Dog who?
Dog poo!

CHLOE FROM GERRARDS CROSS, UK

What travels to different countries but stays in one corner?

A stamp!

SCHLOKA FROM PRINCETON, USA

Why did the elephant sit on a marshmallow?

Because he was afraid he would sink in the hot chocolate!

ADLER FROM SOUTH VIENNA, USA

Knock, Knock!
Who's there?
Me!
Me who?
Me, seriously guys it's me, LET ME IN!

ANAYA FROM WOKINGHAM, UK

What kind of tree fits in your hand?

A palm tree!

BENJAMIN FROM FRESNO, U

Knock, Knock!
Who's there?
Ach!
Ach who?
Bless you!

MAX FROM COULSDON, UK

Why did the cow go this way?

Because he didn't like the "udder" way!

What do you call a balloon shaped like a sausage?
A meat up!

Look at me– I'm turning into a giraffe!
I've never heard such a tall story!

Where do fish eat dinner?
At a pool table!

 **It's unbearable – everywhere I go I hear this screaming noise!**
Please can you ask your little girl to wait outside?

What do you call a cow in love?
Smoo-chy!

How do farmers begin every joke?
Stop me if you've herd this one!

 **When's the worst time to do weight lifting?**
On a weak day!

Why did the man with the wooden leg run away from the playground?
He was afraid of the see-saw!

What's the key to a great Christmas Day?
A tur-key!

Did you hear about the man who was caught stealing bedding?
Police said it was a typical pillow case!

How does a fish with a broken fin get around?

In an eelchair!

DOCTOR, DOCTOR!

I can't stand it – my husband snores with his mouth hanging open! What should I do?

Tell him to put a sock in it!

How should you sit when you're angry?

Cross-legged!

How does a dinosaur like his carrots?
ROAR!

Who's the greediest creature in the forest?
A goblin!

How does an elephant travel?
By jumbo jet!

What do you call a farmer's funny stories?
Pig-tales!

Who has a wand and loves roller coasters?
A whizz-ard!

DOCTOR, DOCTOR! ✚ **It's so strange –
I feel like a horse!**
Are you taking me for
a ride?

**Why did the boy make a mess when he
put his coat on?**
It was a coat of paint!

**Knock
Knock!** Who's there?
Icy!
Icy who?
**Icy your front garden
needs weeding again!**

**Waiter, waiter!
There's a worm in my pasta!**
That's not a worm, sir, it's just a lively
piece of spaghetti.

**My fingers are so
stiff I can't even
open the garden
gate.**
I'm sure you'll get
over it!

What do you call a broken pencil?
Pointless!

DOCTOR, DOCTOR!

Since I arrived I've had this terrible pain in my foot!
Try moving your chair leg!

What did the sheep say when she saw the field of green grass?
Yippee - it's all ewe can eat!

How does an artist clean her teeth?
With a paint brush!

 **I feel so confused, like a bucket of odd socks!**
Book an appointment with the nurse. He'll soon sort you out!

What do you call a bee that can't decide?
A may-bee!

Which farm animal can open a door?
A battering ram!

Where does a bus go when it rains?
To a bus shelter!

Waiter, waiter! This meat is tough!

Keep your voice down, sir – the chef is even tougher!

Which cup is no good for hot drinks?

A buttercup!

[Silly joke alert!] Which pudding makes your dog better? Yoghurt, of course!

How do you catch a falling ice cream?
In a cor-net!

What's the cheapest ring you can buy?
String!

How do cows play hide and seek?
Cam-moo-flage!

What did one butcher say to the other?
Pleased to meat you!

Knock Knock! Who's there?
Water!
Water who?
Water you doing, let me in!

...a boy with a red tummy?
Robin!

...a boy with legs like sticks?
Woody!

...a girl who jingles when she walks?
Isabella!

...a boy that lives across town?
Myles!

...a girl who loves danger?
Amber!

...a boy who takes your car away?
Parker!

Which flower gives you hiccups?
Poppy!

Knock Knock! Who's there?
Wire!
Wire who?
**Wire you taking so
long to open the door?**

**What's the best way to do origami
in the dark?**
Blindfold!

**Why do dragons eat
candles?**
They melt in the mouth!

DOCTOR, DOCTOR! ✚

Every time I go outside I get goose pimples on my ankles!
Oh, do pull your socks up!

How do grizzlies eat their food?
With their bear hands!

Knock, Knock!
Who's there?
Wool ewe!
Wool ewe who?
**Wool ewe open the door, it's freezing
out there!**

**How does a cobbler tell his
children to go away?**
Shoo!

What do you call a dirty bee?
Disgus-sting!

How do sheep play tricks?
They pull the wool over your eyes!

Which bell never rings?
A bluebell!

**What did Humpty Dumpty say as
he hit the ground?**
I'm cracking up!

**What's white, eight feet long and
might just fit through your letterbox?**
Goalpost!

Knock, Knock!
Who's there?
Justin!
Justin who?
**Justin time,
I need the toilet!**

Where should you keep your underpants?

In the bottom drawer!

Who's there?
Shhhh!
Shhhh who?
Don't tell me to go away,
I live here!

Why couldn't the pilot see the controls?
Because he had forgotten to turn on the
flight switch!

What do you call a pixie in a wig?
A hairy fairy!

Why did the frog catch the bus?
His lily pad had been toad away!

WHO WANTS TO HEAR WEE JOKES?

What do you call a wee in the night?
Sleep-pee!

What do you call a toilet queue?
Grum-pee!

**What do you call
a ghost that
goes to the toilet?**
Cree-pee!

What do you call a zebra wee?
Stripe-pee!

What do call a wee on a pancake?
Syrup-pee!

What do you call a bad-tempered cow?
Moo-dy!

What do you call a nosy bee?
A buzzy-body!

 **Which animal fits under a low bridge?**
Duck!

Where does a musician keep their music?
In a notebook!

Which card game do crocodiles play?
Snap!

Why was the sleepy little boy arrested
For kid napping!

Why are pig farmers rude?
They always hog the road!

What do you call a cow on scales?
The Milky Weigh!

What do you call a cow with antlers that goes 'quack'?
Laugh-a-bull!

What do you call a cow that won't share?
Horri-bull!

What do you call a cow that can limbo?
Flexi-bull!

What do you call a cow you won in a bet?
A gam-bull!

What do you call a cow that's afraid of Paddington?
Unbear-a-bull!

What do you call a cow with wings?
Flapp-a-bull!

What do you call a cow that tells you the hay is stale and the barn is cold?
A grum-bull!

And finally, what do you call a cow that's great at football?
Drib-bull!

Why was the flight so bumpy?
It was a flight of steps!

What's the first thing a woodcutter needs to do when he starts work?
See saw!

Help! I think I'm going blind! I can't see anything!
I'm sorry Madam, can you tell your little boy to turn the light back on?

How do horses shout hello?
Hay!

Now it's your turn!

Writing jokes is easy, isn't it? You just think of something funny!

But that gets a bit tricky because people laugh at different things. But if you make up a joke that gets most people chuckling, you've got a good one.

Would you like the chance to show the world how hilarious you are? Here's how to do it!

If you already have a humdinger, then read on. But if you fancy writing your own and you like drawing too, then get your thinking cap on, your pencils ready, and turn to page 58!

What's your best joke?

Send me your greatest joke and I'll put it on my **World Map of Awesome Jokes**!

Head over to the map now to discover silly jokes, clever jokes and weird jokes. Some jokes rhyme, some are a crime, but they're all sent in by children like you!

Will you be first on the map from your town?

Put your awesome joke here at
www.matwaugh.co.uk/jokemap

Write a Bug Joke!

Could you write and illustrate your own joke?

Here's how it works. Start with a great word: **humbug**. In Britain, a humbug is a type of hard, minty sweet or candy (yummy).

But what does humbug *sound* like? A joke!

What do you call an insect that doesn't know the words?
A humbug!

And if you can make a word rhyme, you can make lots *more* jokes! To find rhymes, go through the alphabet to find sounds. Don't forget that some are made up of more than one letter, like **cr**-, **ch**- and **th**-. Let's try it

out with the word humbug, changing the
first sound each time:

a) ➤ nope, I can't make this letter work!

b) ➤ **b**umbug. Oops, I made a rude word! I
won't use that one or I'll be in trouble!

c) ➤ **cr**umbug. That's good! Let me think...

> **What do you call an insect that
> drops its food on the table?**
> A crumbug!

d) ➤ **d**umbug. There's another! What type of
insect would this be?

Now try some more letters. How many jokes
can you make? When you're ready, turn over...

How did you get on? Have you invented a funny bug and a joke to go with it?

Great! Now every awesome joke needs a fantastic illustration, just like the ones in this book by super-clever Yurko. Look at all the detail in his pictures!

Ready? Use the page opposite to tell your bug joke and don't forget to make that drawing really funny!

Happy? Ask a grown-up to take a picture and send it to jokes@matwaugh.co.uk – I'll put all the best ones on the **Wall Of Awesome Jokes** on my website.

Need a bigger sheet to draw on? Go to matwaugh.co.uk/wall

My Awesome Joke!

What do you call...

_____

_____

_____

Answer: _____

My illustration:

first name: _____ **Age:** _____

me town and country: _____

Did you know that rabbits
are born blind? You're
obviously not a baby rabbit.
Have a carrot!

Phew, we're done!

Reviews of joke books are almost as funny as the books themselves.

You're not funny!
These jokes are too old!
These jokes are for babies!
These jokes are too rude!

I get all of those and I don't mind: everyone is different! But if you have something nice to say, or you're just really funny – then please pop over to Amazon with your parent and write something about this book so others know what to expect.

As long as you found something to laugh about in this book, I'm happy too!

Mat

About Mat Waugh

In the first book, I told you about my batty aunt. Here are some new things about me.

I have big crow's feet. I know what you're thinking – how do I buy my shoes? But crow's feet are those wrinkles that grown-ups get next to their eyes.

Some people get them because they need glasses but don't wear them enough (true).

Some people get crow's feet because their skin doesn't have enough oil, called sebum. This may be true, but I only included this fact because I like that word *see-bum*.

But I get crow's feet because I spend hours squinting at my three children, trying to give them Paddington hard stares.

've jumped out of a plane, done bungee jumps and tried wreck diving. I even met Mrs Waugh at a theme park. But last week I got dizzy on the trampoline. The lesson? **Never get old, children!**

still can't do handstands. I'm practising.

've taken a photo of my daughters every single Sunday since they were born. I'm very proud of this, as I'm not very good at homework. In nearly every photo, they're pulling a silly face at me.

inally, I love getting emails (but ask your parents!) mail@matwaugh.co.uk

Three more to try!

Cheeky Charlie vol 1-6

Meet Harriet and her small, stinky brother. Together, they'r trouble. Fabulously funny stories for kids aged 6 and up.

Fantastic Wordsearches

Wordsearch with a difference: themed, crossword clues and hidden words await!

What's the Magic Word?

It's Alfie's birthday, but it's not going to plan! If only he could remember the magic word - ca you help him? For forgetful children aged 4+.

Available from Amazon and local bookshops.

Be the first to know about new stuff! Sign up for my emails at matwaugh.co.uk

Made in the USA
Lexington, KY
01 December 2019